THE MELANCHOLY LIFE OF DORIS MENNING

R. Nikolas Macioci

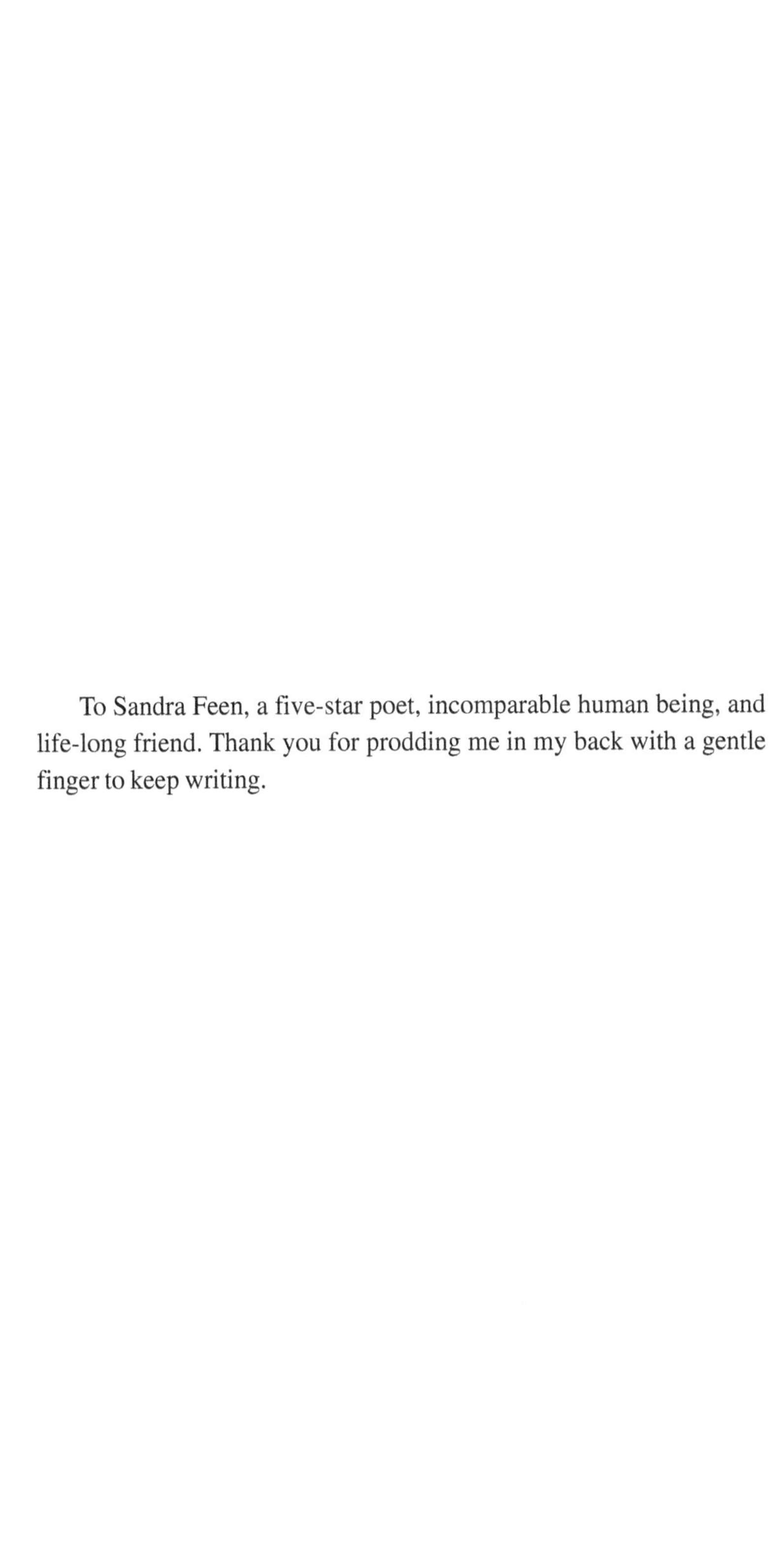

To Sandra Feen, a five-star poet, incomparable human being, and life-long friend. Thank you for prodding me in my back with a gentle finger to keep writing.

ACKNOWLEDGEMENTS

The Clark Street Review   "Doris Observes a Couple at the Bistro"

The Clark Street Review   "Doris Finally Connects"

The Clark Street Review   "Doris Deceived"

Tipton Poetry Journal   "Doris as a Third Grader"

Jonah Magazine "Doris Imagines a Relationship in the Grocery Store"

Jonah Magazine   "Doris at the Holy Bird Bar"

Maybe true love isn't out there for me, but I
can sublimate my loneliness with the
notion that true love is out there for
someone.

Roxane Gay

Loneliness and the feeling of being
unwanted is the most terrible poverty.

Mother Teresa

Contents

DORIS AS A THIRD GRADER

"Come sit with me," her father says. "We'll go
 over your times tables." She rises from
the living room floor where she has been cutting
paper dolls, pulls a stool next to her dad.
"I'll say the problem, and you give the answer."
He is patient as God and more important
to her than any of her dolls. "You're very
good with numbers," he tells her. She smiles.

Her mother appears in the doorway, howling
about Doris not cleaning her room, needing
to get ready for bed, and that he is spoiling her
with too much attention.

Her father tells her to put away
the multiplication chart and prepare
for bed. "You're too soft with her,"
the mother screeches.

Doris climbs steps to the bathroom, brushes
her teeth, stands looking in the mirror,
feels an aversion to her own reflection.
She turns off the light, slumps to her bed,
gets in, and hugs her Disney princess doll.

Outside, snow blows past the window
and under the security light like
a stream of unwanted white ants.

DORIS OBSERVES A COUPLE AT THE BISTRO

He is already loved by the woman
with the blank face and moist mouth. Doris
can tell from ten yards away that this
woman's thoughts are as shapeless as stars.
Doris strains to hear their voices, deep
and secret. They struggle to keep anyone
from listening to their romantic patter.
Later, when no one is around, she will glide
into his arms again and again, her actions
timid, his, a thousand kinds of attention.
Doris is breakable in here, thinking
she would die for their apparent happiness,
for their dance toward fulfillment. Her wedding
ring glitters when she moves a hand, his too
is alive with light. They fold their napkins
carelessly and head to where they will listen
to sounds only their bodies will hear,
clinging, delicate sounds away from a third
person's ears, barred from everything
Doris knows will happen.

DORIS AT THE HOLY BIRD BAR

She's sipping a margarita when he
sits down at the next table with his back
to her. He's wearing gray slacks, plain
twill tweed sport coat and shirt as white
as marshmallow. Her eyes keep going
to his neck as if to study its anatomy:
muscles, ligaments, tendons, but she is
staring at visible skin and hair touching
the collar. To change focus and distract
herself, she looks around at Art Deco
glass, chrome, stainless steel, shiny fabrics,
streamlined geometric forms. Everywhere
she looks leads back to his neck. The
fascination defies ordinary explanation.
She wants to touch him, but it's more,
it's desire magnified, sensual need at
her fingertips, the object of symbolic lust.
Again, she attempts to look elsewhere
at the lacquered bar, inlaid wood, mirrors,
clean lines that bring her back again to his
neck. What if he turned around? Would
she feel the same? He finishes his drink
and leaves which breaks the spell. By
herself, she still imagines stroking his
hair, feeling her hand against his neck
like a hymn to passion.

DORIS FINALLY CONNECTS

She stuffs a five-dollar bill under the waistband
of his briefs. The briefs are a skimpy suggestion.
He's not a Greek god, but he could be the brother
of one, lean as if he hadn't eaten for a month,
skin flawless and smooth as a flower petal.
He's danced to "Gangsta's Paradise," leaves
the stage to mingle with patrons of Pleasure Palace
night club. Doris returns to her seat at the bar.
She's wearing navy shorts, a haymaker
elbow-sleeve Henley, and a bob cut. She catches
his eye, and his glance lingers. Next thing,
he's beside her. She offers to buy him a drink.
He tells her he wants to dress first, and he'll
be back. Alone, she doesn't think he'll return,
but he does, his immaculate body barely
hidden beneath red denim shorts and a white
t-shirt. He accepts a Jack and Coke. She's
taking small mouthfuls of a margarita. They
exchange names. Bill's arm brushes the soft
skin of her arm. They small talk into closing
hours. Later, they lie down in her bed,
heartbeats evenly matched, mutual hunger
merging, a stranger's touch slicing through
thirty years of solitude.

DORIS DISCOVERS SOME TRUTHS

Slipping in and out of each other's arms
all night, she questions his attraction
to her, a man twenty years her junior,
jokes about being his mom, teases with
"Have you figured out yet that I'm too
old for you?" Bill says no and turns his
pillow. In morning light, she has not
misjudged his perfection. His face
is a male Madonna. They know very
little about each other after only a
one-night stand.

She cooks breakfast: eggs, bacon, toast,
asks if he needs a lift to work, since he
has no car. "I'm waiting for a job
opening," he says. "Right now, I'm dancing
a couple nights a week." She can't believe
he can subsist on that, and red flags go up.
She's retired with a guaranteed income.
Is he a gigolo or just a guy between jobs?
"Can I take you home?" she asks. He answers
"Three other guys are letting me live with them
for the moment." Another red flag goes up
like hot neon. Though dismayed by his
shortcomings, she agrees to a second date
and drives him to where he's staying.
Returning home, she feels hollow.

DORIS RECOGNIZES WHAT SILENCE MEANS

Before her second date with Bill, she rummages
through piles of clothes, trying to pick an outfit.
Denim skirt, white t-shirt with Levi's
seem perfect for a casual outing.

When Bill opens her car door, his Levi's ride low,
t-shirt inky black. Soon his head is leaning against
the side window, mouth open as if asleep.
He's a corpse with no conversation. They
roll into Zack's Pizza, order, and wait.

He says nothing, and she thinks so this is
what it's like finally to be in a romantic
relationship. Though he sits across from
her, she feels empty as a room everyone
has left. Boldly she asks, "Are you high?"
He answers no, but his tongue is cottony,
his eyes half closed.

He looks at a clock on the wall shaped like a Coke
bottle and asks, "Do you have a few bucks I can
borrow?" She digs into her purse, retrieves
fifteen dollars, shoves it across the table.
"How do you plan on paying me back?
You're jobless and without a car." He stares
at her, blinks. "I'm working on something,"
he answers.

Has she purchased him, fallen for an indigent?
They eat in silence, leave, and she drops him
where he's staying. On the drive home, her hands
grip the wheel. She suspects her mistake, and
regret begins to howl through her like a Chicago wind.

DORIS DECEIVED

Their one night of passion lasts only
as long as a pastry, sweet, momentary.
Bill scarcely speaks, hastens to dress
like an efficient lover, lights a cigarette,
asks if she's ready to take him home.
She's startled by his impatience, his
restlessness to leave. At the door, she
pokes around in her purse for keys,
discovers missing cash, pretends
not to notice.

In the car, he presses against the door
as if to escape. She doesn't mention
money, apprehensive of his reaction.
Bill asks if she would like to see him
again. They stop, exchange numbers
on paper scraps. He doesn't attempt
an intimate goodbye, blows out a stream
of smoke, and says, "I'll see ya"

As she drives home, she's rigid with anger
at his thievery, not confronting
him. She gambled on a casual encounter,
got a destitute gigolo. Her mouth is dry,
her heart empty. He looted her loneliness.

DORIS'S INTERLUDE

What she wants will probably never happen,
so she washes clothes, rings water
into the scrub bucket, mops, empties waste baskets,
cuts coupons, counts left-over change.
The face of possibility looks away from hers.
All of her life people have thought of her
as an iceberg, someone alone
in the moonlight. Obligations to family
obviated social options like a stone
around her neck. Watching birds wallop birdbath water
or maple trees shrivel leaves in autumn
amounted to her life. Family died,
and her world opened to a single one-night stand.
She offered her solitude to an amateur
opportunist whom she abandoned
like imperfect love. On a stormy night,
she would like to fold into someone's arms,
feel rain river her from inertia and the past.

DORIS IMAGINES A RELATIONSHIP
IN THE GROCERY STORE

It is in her head to meet someone new.
In the Kroger produce department, people
pause to pull plastic bags from spools.
Brussels sprouts, cauliflower, kale drip
with perpetual water. A lean man
in khaki cargo shorts and a green golf
shirt strolls up beside her, reaches for a
head of lettuce, smiles, says hi, and walks
away. She hangs back then follows him,
stays at the top of the cereal aisle
while he grabs Wheaties from a shelf. He
turns, sees her and smiles again. This time,
she wanders past him to the other end
of the aisle and disappears around the corner.
She's embarrassed by brazen boldness, stands
still as if examining ingredients of a potato
chip bag and asks herself what best can come
out of this situation? Her chest hurts
from being desperate, from showing too much
vulnerability. Did she veil her face
with nonchalance? Was her need visible?
He's two lanes down from where she's checking out.
She can see only his head over impulse items.

DORIS ARRIVES AT LAKESIDE

She knows nothing about traveling alone,
has never been on a vacation without
family, but loves the idea of peering
into a pamphlet and one morning
wandering off. She's packed one suitcase
and an overnight bag, enough not to
be overburdened with luggage.

From Columbus it's two and a half hours
to Lakeside, Ohio. Her blue Elantra
speeds along I-71. She's content in being
part of a plan. Though leaves linger, there
are signs of autumn at their edges as she
passes groves of trees and numerous
cornfields.

The last week of August embezzles daylight,
but she turns through the gate of Lakeside
with enough daylight left to explore. Something
in her wants a casual release. All her life
she has used the language of denial, a misstep
in the business of living. For the time
being, she is renting a life as well as a cabin.
Shouldering her purse, she heads out
on foot, making room in her heart for
occasional joy and unexpected love.

DORIS LINGERS AT LAKESIDE

She saunters among lavish, extensive
flower gardens: aster, lavender, dahlia,
pansies, and orchids comprise a profusion
of hues and tints. Sky pours out unblemished
blue of larkspur.

In Hoover auditorium she studies an art
exhibit, thinks how hard it would be to judge.
Heritage Hall Museum, Herb Garden Lakeview
Historic Inn occupy her afternoon. She strolls
hand in hand with the sun, a goldfish transformed
into a sphere.

Lunch at Sloopy's Sports Cafe and dinner
at Hotel Lakeside dining room slip her into
evening and one of a dozen rocking chairs
on the hotel's porch facing Lake Erie.
Sunset spreads a hundred shades of pink
on the horizon. She rocks, watching
people around her laughing with faces
full of happiness.

Three chairs down, a man, maybe a few years
older than she, cares enough to smile. His
teeth are beautiful, eyes green as serpentine.
For no reason, she says hello. He moves
down a chair. Moon is starting to make a trail
across water like a map for romance. They
exchange amenities. His name is Nelson,
and he discloses his interest in tennis,
says he played all day. Before he leaves,
he suggests that maybe their paths will cross again.
She is warmed by the possibility of escaping
the solitude of another unescorted day.

DORIS REMAINS AT LAKESIDE

She orders breakfast in the hotel
dining room, something simple like orange
juice and a croissant. Soon, a shadow
overlays her table, and the tennis player
from the previous night asks if he may
join her. This morning, she notices gray
in his sideburns that flank a full head
of mahogany hair. They talk of their
schedules, his tennis match, and her plans
to visit the Fine Print bookstore. They
agree to meet for dinner.

Sun's heat is stubborn as a donkey, boiling
downward and unmoving, but the day is
about bathing and boats. She ambles to
the dock where gulls squawk and scrap
for food. Swimmers splash as if they wore
fins, float, paddle, make transparent
water sparks above their heads.

They meet at five. She's hungry for a
conversation that will lead them closer.
She orders lamb salad with fregola. He
asks for scallop sashimi with meyer lemon
confit. He's retired from civil engineering
that designs highways. She was a high school
math teacher. His wife danced cancer.
She's never been married.

Slowly, they move to the Hotel's front porch
rocking chairs and then his suite. Inside his
room with his hand under her chin, he tips
her head back.

DORIS DESERTED

Doris awakens amidst the elaborate
Victorian furnishings of Hotel Lakeside,
thinks instantly of Miss Havisham's house
in *Great Expectations* and of the fact
that she is alone. Looking around the room,
she sees no evidence of an occupant.
The man who brought her here is gone, so are
clothes, suitcase, toiletries. She had hoped
the man named Nelson was more than an aged
playboy. She checks the rooms once more, craves clues
that he hasn't abandoned her.

Showered and dressed, she sits stunned in the sumptuous
dining room, a glass of orange juice in front
of her. Was it a mistake to travel
to this resort alone only to feel
like a cast- off orphan?

Rather than return to her motel room
four miles away, she resolves to resist
despair and spend the day here at Lakeside.

Lake Erie sparkles in sunlight like a watery,
diamond necklace. Children and teenagers
rollick and romp in the pool where water
is turquoise blue. She is calm as morning
light, refusing melancholy and to be
someone on the opposite side of happiness.
She lingers on a bench amid shasta daisies
and marigolds, deeply patient to ever hear
I love you.

DORIS IN LIMBO

She touches up the gray in her hair, wears
a little heavier makeup, seeks underlit
places when in public. She trips over
her own life that's underfoot, laments
that her hands seem more veined. Feeling
as if she's already buried, she climbs out
of her grave each day a little more wrinkled,
withered. Everywhere she looks, pure
faces of the young peer back.
"Let me pull you aside," she says under
her breath, "and tell you how dreams fail
and how life without love suffocates."
Rebellion against crumbling flesh weakens
her. Worst, opportunity weighs against time
as she waits on the far side of middle age.

Darkening days of winter accentuate her
loneliness, wound the already wounded.
Why hasn't anyone found her pretty
as the sea, profound as surf? Sad to have
fallen for a man more in love with himself
than anyone else, who ambled into her
solitude drunk on deception. Now, she
must decalcify her heart, forgive herself
for losing it to the wrong man.

DORIS AT THE END OF THE DAY

Autumn light slants through French doors,
lies across the baby grand piano like a
saffron friend. Her fingers curve
into Gabriel Faure's *Payane*. Nostalgic
notes slide from her hands like melodic
daydreams, echo through the room and
into the hall. Her heart drifts on a river
of sound. When she approached the piano,
she had thought she wanted to die, but
playing a mosaic of music mollified
anxiety and her failure at love, the
unfinished poem of her solitary life.
She listens to the house sing its song
of nearly a hundred years of fieldstone
masonry, childhood memories.

Finished playing, she turns toward the doors
behind her. Red and yellow leaves graze glass
like stiff paint brushes. At fifty-four
she shies away from the world
toward anonymity, harbors an elegant
sanity about unhappiness. It walks with her
near the stone wall that surrounds the house,
reaches out in the night to comfort unlike
any man. Her inner voice tells her
to be patient with the human heart, that
everything grows from thinking nothing
will happen.